They will not open their eyes before they are at least three weeks old

There is a lot of excitement around the otter den in early spring. The home that the otters choose is often one that a muskrat or beaver used in the years before. Though this den could be beneath the roots of a tree or in a very thick brush pile, the favorite home would be dug into a bank by a stream, lake, pond or marsh.

Up to six little otter cubs can be born in early spring, but usually there are only two or three. They are born with their eyes closed and will not open their eyes before they are at least three weeks old. They begin to feed on their mother's rich milk and grow very fast.

*O*tters are shy animals and need plenty of room to swim, eat and raise their families. They need healthy water like a clear mountain lake, deep rushing river or a marsh filled with life. The otter is most active from early evening until early morning but it is not that unusual for an otter to be seen throughout the day.

Next to their skin are very short, thick hairs and covering those hairs are dark, coarse guard hairs that the otter constantly cleans and oils to make certain that he stays waterproof and warm. A very important part of the way an otter is made is that he has little "flaps" or valves in his nose and ears. When he goes under the water, those flaps close to keep the water out. The little otter is perfectly equipped to spend his life in and out of the water.

The otter is perfectly equipped
to spend his life in water

The youngsters will not go in the water at first...

The mother otter is a very good parent and spends lots of time caring for and teaching her babies how to survive in their new home. After about eight weeks she will take them to the water to show them the world that will become their own. The youngsters are not willing to go in the water at first so she may have to take them by the fur on their neck and pull them to the water's edge. Her best way of teaching them to swim is to ride them along on her back and occasionally go under the water leaving the little one dog-paddling on the surface. Soon she comes up underneath him and carries him again on her back until soon he swims away on his own. Since an otter must learn to love the water, this gentle introduction allows the little guy to be a happy swimmer without any fear of the water at all.

*M*any people find the otter a funny looking little animal. He is a member of the weasel family that includes the mink, skunk and badger. His body is long and slender and his nose is wide and hairless with lots of bristle-like whiskers. With short, stubby legs and webbed feet with five toes on each foot, the otter is quite a sight when he stops to pose in his wilderness world. He can weigh between 15 and 25 pounds and from nose to tail, otters are three to four feet long. All of these special features make him the best swimmer of all animals because he can use his foot long tail and webbed feet to move through the water very quickly.

...the otter is quite a sight,
               when he stops to pose

When it comes to fishing, the otter is very interesting

Fish make up the largest part of the otter's food but he will eat most anything that he can catch including the second most favorite food, the crayfish. Bird eggs, snakes and frogs are some of the other foods that an otter likes. When it comes to catching a fish, an otter is probably the most interesting of all animals. In clear water he is quick and may approach a fish from the bottom and either catch it in his mouth or in his sharp little claws. He has a third eyelid that is clear and while it protects his eye from the cold water, he can see through it. In the darker colored waters of marshes and ponds, the otter cannot rely on his sight so he turns to the very sensitive whiskers on his broad little face. They are so sensitive that he can feel the movement of a fish nearby and can react fast enough to catch it. One other important thing about the otter is that he can catch fish at night by looking closely at the bottom. Since a fish must move to stay in the same place in the flow of water, the light reflects off his scales and the otter finds his food that way.

The otter is actually a friend to the fisherman

*M*any people who like to fish once thought that the otter was not their friend. They thought that he would probably eat lots of fish that people like to catch (like the trout and the salmon). After studying the otter for many years it turns out that he is actually a friend to the fisherman. He eats the slow, rough fish that few people like to eat. Since these fish sometimes crowd out the good fish like the trout, it turns out that the otter really improves the stream for everyone to enjoy.

An otter may travel up to five miles a day when he hunts up and down the river or through the marsh or around his home in the lake. He loves to play in the water and he is often seen rolling and tumbling with other otters. He comes on to land often to mark his territory on rocks and stumps. Other otters can then tell by their great sense of smell how old the otter is, whether it is a male or female otter, and even how healthy the otter is that left his scent. The scent is so different in each otter that it is like our fingerprint.

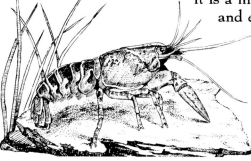

...they shake as much water as
they can out of their oily f...

When an otter goes underwater, he can stay under for several minutes and because he swims so well, he can travel a long distance under the water. After he comes to the top of the water, he is very hard to see. His dark coat is even darker when wet and since his eyes are conveniently located on the top of his head, he swims with most of his body under the water. He glides along in the water with very little effort, often rolling up and down or diving down for a rock and tossing it out in front of him, then diving to catch it again. Otters often travel in groups of two or more and seem to enjoy the playful ways of the other otters.

When they come out of the water, they shake as much water as they can out of their oily fur. After shaking, they find a favorite "drying spot" where they roll and rub until they have cleaned their shiny coat. They use these drying spots over and over throughout the season unless these spots are covered in snow.

...the otter loves to run and slide

The river otter is a very smart little animal. He has lots of games that teach him to be fast and strong. His favorite game is the slide. Along a muddy bank or on a grassy slope, the otter loves to run and slide then climb back up the hill and slide again. Though he might prefer to play with the other otters, he can entertain himself and play alone for hours. Often the thing that interrupts his play is a sound or smell that seems new or different. His ears are small but he can hear very well and his sense of smell is also very good. Because he is so curious, he will stop everything that he is doing and inspect a noise or the smell of another animal in his territory.

Otters know that they cannot catch too much food in a small area of their territory or the food could run out so they travel long distances to hunt. Their territory in summer may include as much as fifty to seventy miles of lakes and streams. It can take as much as two weeks to travel and hunt that area. The otter seems to know where to find food as he travels back and forth across his wilderness world.

Mom had to teach him to love the water...

A lot has happened to the baby otter in a very short amount of time. His mom had to teach him to love the water. Sometimes she has caught a small fish or a frog and let the little otter play with it before she lets it go in the water so he will chase it. He was really awkward when he first started swimming at about two months of age, but in just six months he can take care of himself. He will stay with his mom for almost a year or until she has more cubs. The mother will then encourage her young cubs to look after themselves and they may travel twenty miles looking for the right home. As they travel, they swim in a nearly straight line to cover the greatest distance in a short amount of time. When they need to eat, they hunt by zigzagging across the water in search of any tasty fish below them.

He will roll and toss in the fresh snow...

*I*n winter the river otter stays very active to keep warm. He can lose his body heat very fast in cold water, so he spends lots of time cleaning his fur so that his waterproof hair will keep out the cold. Just beneath his two coats of fur he has a very warm layer of fat that also protects him in the winter. He will roll and toss in the fresh snow to stay clean and dry. When he catches a fish he will be very careful that his enemies like the wolf, lynx or bobcat are not near his feeding area.

Otters make lots of very interesting sounds. When frightened he may chirp or when playing he may chatter. If he is defending his territory against other otters he can growl and when he is happy he grunts. Baby otters make a noise that sounds like a chuckle. Even in winter the otter will play for hours until hunger forces him to look for food.

Sliding is a very good way to move across the snow...

Wintertime travel from one feeding spot to another is a good use of some of the lessons that the otter has learned from playing. While moving across his snow-covered home range, the otter will make several long bounds followed by a flop on his belly and a slide of ten feet or more. He seems to love this type of travel and repeats these steps often. It is a very good way to move across the snow and like many other parts of the otter's daily life, it seems a lot like play. The journey in winter often leads to a waterfall or some cascading rapids. The constant movement of the water keeps the ice from freezing solid and the otter can catch the fish that gather in the bubbling waters.

...it seems a lot like play

No other animal seems to get so much pleasure out of life

Our friend the otter asks very little from us in order to be the happy little fellow that he is. He must have clean water, good food, and few disturbances from people. No other animal seems to get so much pleasure out of life as the otter. Remember that everyday as someone walks through a meadow and along a clear running stream or canoes through a marsh making very little sound, the otter is watching. He may even come to greet you. If you take the time to watch, he may even perform for you. What a wonderful wilderness world we still have to enjoy. It is good to know that the otter is doing much better these days thanks to folks like you who are learning more about him. When you think about all the things that you love in the great outdoors, save a thought and a smile for the river otter, our happiest animal in the wild.